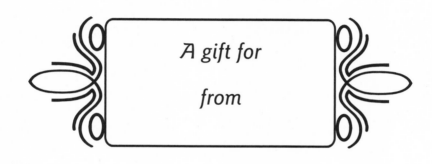

A gift for

from

50 Ways to Love Your Mother

Gift Ideas for Aging Parents and Others When All They Need Is Love

Jane Monachelli, M.A., L.P.C.

A Golden Gift Guide from
Helping House Phoenix, Arizona

HELPING
HOUSE

Publisher's Cataloging-in-Publication Data

Monachelli, Jane.
    50 ways to love your mother : gift ideas for aging parents and others when all they need is love / by Jane Monachelli. — 1st ed. — Phoenix, Ariz. : Helping House, 2006.
    p. ; cm.
    ISBN-13: 978-09777721-4-8
    "A Golden Gift Guide."
Includes bibliographical references.
    1. Gifts. 2. Older people—Care. 3. Self-esteem in old age.
I. Title. II. Fifty ways to love your mother.
    GT3040 .M66 2006
    394—dc22 0604

Helping House
17 E. Orange Dr.
Phoenix AZ 85012-1427
(602) 234-0907
Info@50waystolove.com

For updates on products and company contact information, please visit our Web site at www.50waystolove.com

Dedication

For Will and Sammy

Diddle, Diddle!

Table of Contents

Acknowledgments

I wish to thank and acknowledge the following people who have been a blessing in my life and on this project:

Family, including:

My beloved husband, Ron, my precious son, Brad, and my cherished daughter-in-law, Lisa

My heart sister and first cousin, Nancy McCorkle

My cousin-in-law, Suzanne Schutt

My sister-in-law, Mary Margaret Hickman

And *the* Uncle Jimmy and his sweet sister Anne

And with *special honor*, my mentor, godmother, Sunday school teacher, Girl Scout leader, namesake, choir director, piano teacher and Aunt, Jane Page Menefee Schutt

And with *special love*, my dear departed mother and father, Lou and Bill Hickman, and Uncle Wallie

Friends, including the "Breakfast Club"—Deanna Delmar, Maggie, Dorris, Carol Sadler, Kay Jones—and Laurene Griest and Moncia Zontanos, Patti Cobleigh, Marilyn Roelse, Kay Burkhart, Robin Dilley, Nan Perkins, Janet and Manny Burruel, Marge Ebling, Chris Hughes, Ann Holloman, Lynne Lewis, Judy Preble, Pat Browne, Christie Dater, Theresa Gerbig, Carolyn Phillips, Mary Davies

And with *special love and honor*, my dearest pal and cohort, Kay Loy Payne

Teachers, including Genie Zieger and Forrest Ashby, Lib Allison

Consultant and person without whom the project would have never gone from my dreams to a reality, Mary Westheimer

Also Angela Amitrano-Sawalquah and Eileen Szychowski, Terry Gibbs and John Kremer for their invaluable help along the way to publication

Thanks are due, too, to Linda Strauss Lewis for her lovely illustrations and to Gwen Henson of SageBrush Publications for the book's beautiful design. Together, they caught the spirit of the book and translated it physically into a work of art, making it better than it would have been without them.

Finally, thanks to all of the caregivers—sons, daughters, nieces, nephews, students, admirers and those professionals—who give so much of themselves in caring for others.

Introduction

As my mother entered her "golden years," I lived far away from her. She was in Mississippi, and I was in Arizona. Yet I longed to help her to feel loved and special, especially because a person's journey from independence to loss and limits is often a rough one.

Frustration was my companion as I struggled to think of lovely things that would help her know she was thought of and cared about each day. She had very little room in the care center she'd moved into, and each change in her situation brought about less physical space and storage. She didn't need any more *things*; in fact she always seemed to need to be getting rid of things. This situation only seemed to underscore the growing list of losses.

Yet ideas started coming together in my mind as the journey progressed. As I helped her visit and interview for the care center where she would spend her last five years, I noticed that residents who got a lot of attention from their families seemed to receive special status and prestige. My mother needed and deserved such attention and respect. Fortunately, she had her son and his wife, and her precious twin granddaughters and grandson nearby, as they impacted her life with visits and calls and gatherings that brought obvious joy to her days. She was blessed with many good friends who were loyal and attentive. She also continued to attend and be involved in her church, which was a source of strength and renewal.

In spite of these blessings, there were still lonely days and times when she seemed to long for affirmation that she *mattered*. My project began as a way to let her know that she was important and loved at this hard stage of her life.

My dear friend Kay Payne was also going through this process as her dad moved to a care center in North Carolina. She and I would brainstorm and look for clever ideas. We talked with residents at some of the care centers to hear directly what they felt was the best or most helpful gift they had received. We gained tremendously from this research.

We also learned a lot simply by watching others in our position. For example, my mother's best friend had a planned outing with her daughter each week. This classy lady also had a chauffeur for the extremely hard time when she had to give up driving, as nearly all of our aging loved ones do at some point. I loved this idea, but my challenge was to find a way to replicate some of these gestures of love for those of us without the benefit of a similar budget and proximity.

Indeed, I discovered many resources and ideas that helped my own mother, as well as my dear Aunt Jane, and my enigmatic Uncle Jimmy, manage these times in their lives. Eventually, I decided to put them in a little book to help others with this same challenge. There are ordinary as well as perfectly lovely ideas that are not listed here, such as writing a letter to your loved one. (I saw my own mother, at a fragile 82, jump for joy and exclaim, "A handwritten letter!" as we departed her mailbox one day.) This book attempts to go beyond the obvious and wonderful gestures to give you ideas and a creative spark as you love your own aging parent or other elders. This volume is also intended to take into account the busy pace of our lives, so I have tried to make the ideas doable and easy to fulfill.

I hope this book is helpful to you, and to your friends and relatives, as we travel down this golden road together with our loved ones.

—*Jane Monachelli*

P.S. You may notice that there are more than 50 ideas in the book. I just couldn't help myself—we just can never do enough nice things for our loved ones!

Getting Comfortable at Home

The Big Search

My mother and all of her friends in the care center played a constant game of "let's find"...much to their aggravation. Even in their tiny homes, many things would get lost.

It seemed the most often missing and most aggravating of all lost items were their room keys. This issue came up several times a day, such as when they went to and returned from meals and checking the mail, or any other activity outside their apartments.

We came up with several ideas for addressing this issue. None of them solved the problem altogether, but combined, they went a long way toward preserving everyone's peace of mind.

The first helper is a squiggly plastic cord that is worn on the wrist for keys. This "key keeper" works for both the plastic credit card type as well as traditional metal keys. You can find these at most office supply stores. I found one at a corner UPS Store.

The second is a key rack that is located just inside your loved one's home or room. The rack should be placed as close as possible to the nearest light switch, because that is usually the first stop inside. One attractive version can be found in the Sundance mail-order catalog.

The most dramatic option is a product invented by the company Sharper Image™ called "Now You Can Find It®." This clever remote, which costs about $70, attaches to the key. It sends a signal to the missing key ring, which then beeps and flashes. It can be invaluable—as long as you can locate the remote!

Tip *When my mother's family and friends visited, we learned to ask if she was missing anything that we could help find. Often, she would have misplaced her hearing aid and would be hesitant to tell us out of sheer embarrassment. We took the pressure off her by making it just part of our regular visit to inquire about what was lost and found. The space behind any furniture that is placed against a wall is a good starting point. It's dark and hard to reach so you never know what you'll find.*

key keeper
ⓘ UPS™, www.upsstore.com
ⓘ Also try local office supply stores

Now You Can Find It!
ⓘ Sharper Image, 800-344-4444, www.sharperimage.com

key rack
ⓘ Sundance, 800-422-2770, www.sundancecatalog.com

key keeper
Price: up to $10

Easy if your loved one is
❤ *long distance*
❤ *local*

Pack it yourself

Now You Can Find It!
Price: $61–$100

Easy if your loved one is
❤ *long distance*
❤ *local*

Delivered by retailer

key rack
Price: $26–$60

Easy if your loved one is
❤ *long distance*
❤ *local*

Delivered by retailer

Comfort and Convenience Calling

Being in one locale when your loved one is in another adds to the challenge of caring.

It turned out to be a very big help for me in Arizona to have a phone book from my mother's community in Mississippi. There were many times this allowed me to call her pharmacy, podiatrist or other local provider, or to just send her flowers locally rather than by FTD. I could—and did—call her pastor when I had questions or needs, and I just felt more grounded having her local phone book. Whenever I visited Mother, I would make sure I picked up the latest edition.

Another phone book issue actually surprised me. My mother lived in a city, but one small enough to still have just one phone book. This made the book too heavy for her to handle. We learned to cut it in half and use good old masking tape or duct tape to reinforce its altered binding. She couldn't have cut it herself, and I wasn't very good at it, either, but one of her male friends in the care center was delighted to help with this task.

Tip *When someone in the care center offered help, it was positive in every way to accept. Whether it was doing a little mending as mother's eyesight failed, or cutting the phone book in two, it seemed to make the helper feel good, and we appreciated it, too.*

A Little Help From a Professional

Price: more than $100

Easy if your loved one is
- *long distance*
- *local*

Some of us think we have to do it all ourselves. There are times, however, that a little assistance makes a big difference.

When her mother moved into an apartment at a care center, my friend Frances Mills-Yeager hired an interior decorator. The decorator was able to help her mother think through which of her current possessions would work best in her apartment and help her make better use of the limited space.

Before the move, they spent time at her mother's home choosing items to take along. Then the decorator hung the pictures and arranged the furniture in her new abode.

Somehow this helped make the move less emotional—perhaps having a professional involved in the process added some excitement to it, or simply made it less deeply personal.

Tip *You can find a designer through the phone book, by searching on the Internet, or through the American Society of Interior Designers, Inc.*

ⓘ American Society of Interior Designers, Inc.,
202-546-3480, www.asid.org

The Challenge of a Tiny Kitchen

A major challenge of helping my mother move to the care center was choosing which of her kitchen things to take along. Most of us have a lot of kitchen utensils and appliances, and the apartments in assisted living centers will not accommodate all of our treasures.

We learned that Mother did very little real cooking once settled in this new situation and didn't need much. Such a change was hard for her to imagine, though, as we were making the plans.

A wonderful resource for determining what to take is a delightful book called *The Tiny Kitchen Cooking and Entertaining* (Tiny Kitchen Publishing, 2001) by Denise Sullivan Medved. She provides a list of only 28 items that make a well-stocked kitchen. She offers ideas about storage and provides a collection of recipes for gracious entertaining using these items. If I had known about the book before we made the move, we would have had a much easier time. I could have even looked at Mother's signature recipes and made sure they could be created with these items, and then included just a few more to accommodate her orange chiffon cake or popovers.

As excerpted from *The Tiny Kitchen* with the publisher's permission, here are the recommended supplies for the well-stocked tiny kitchen:

- ❑ 6-inch paring knife
- ❑ 10-inch knife
- ❑ potato peeler
- ❑ rubber spatula
- ❑ pancake turner
- ❑ sieve (doubles as a sifter and a colander)
- ❑ pastry brush
- ❑ steamer (metal)
- ❑ tongs
- ❑ hand eggbeater
- ❑ rolling pin
- ❑ 2-cup glass measuring cup
- ❑ set of measuring spoons
- ❑ cake rack
- ❑ cookie sheet
- ❑ 4-sided grater
- ❑ two 9-inch pie plates
- ❑ 9x13 glass baking dish
- ❑ jelly roll pan (14 1/2 x 10 1/2 x 1 inch)
- ❑ roasting pan
- ❑ broiler pan
- ❑ nest of 4 glass mixing bowls
- ❑ 6-quart stock pot with lid
- ❑ 4-quart saucepan with lid
- ❑ 2-quart saucepan with lid
- ❑ 8x8 square baking pan
- ❑ 10-inch tube cake pan
- ❑ 10-inch skillet

Tip *This book is well worth owning. It also includes a list of prepared foods to have on hand as well as the recipes and the list for a well-stocked kitchen.*

- ⓘ Independent Publishers Group, 800-888-4741, www.ipgbook.com
- ⓘ Amazon.com®, www.amazon.com
- ⓘ Barnes & Noble®, 800-843-2665, www.bn.com
- ⓘ Your local bookstore can order it for you

Price: $10–$25

Easy if your loved one is
- ♥ *long distance*
- ♥ *local*

Delivered by retailer

Pack it yourself

Put It Here

When downsizing from a larger home, space is always precious. Every inch has potential.

Adjustable under-the-sink shelves can provide valuable storage for cleaning supplies, plastic ware and other sturdy belongings. The home improvement store Lowe's® sells one type for about $16. These shelves take into account the pipes under the sink, getting the most out of an out-of-the-way spot.

Shelves and even under-sink trash cans that slide out on tracks from inside cabinets, providing easier access, are also available as kits. The sliding feature makes items easier to see and reduces reach, saving strain on challenged backs and flexibility. Having items easier to view reduces clutter and the waste of repurchasing some things that are just "hiding."

Tip *Always think about storage when you make a purchase for your loved one.*

ⓘ Lowe's, 800-445-6937, www.lowes.com

Price: $10–$25

Easy if your loved one is
♥ *long distance*
♥ *local*

Delivered by retailer

Pack it yourself

Bonus Tip *Delivery and installation of slider kits is now commonly available through larger hardware stores.*

Let's Not Cry Over Spilled Milk

Price: $61–$100

Easy if your loved one is
❤ *long distance*
❤ *local*

Delivered by retailer

When we were growing up, my brother and I were fortunate because "Lou," as everyone called my mother, didn't make a terrible fuss over spills and messes. My brother and his wife returned the favor by providing Mother with an easy-to-use, handheld wet/dry cordless vacuum cleaner.

Even when she lived in the care center and housekeeping was a part of her plan, this appliance was a blessing. At six pounds, it was light enough for her to handle, and any mess could be quickly and easily cleaned up with almost no bother. This particular model is stored in a recharging base, and its superior suction and HEPA filtration system are nice features.

Tip *Always be aware of the weight of any item you choose or send. As people age, the amount of weight they can control diminishes.*

ⓘ Brookstone®, 800-926-7000, www.brookstone.com

Alert and Available

Peace of mind can be a priceless gift for loved ones, and for you and your family. Especially valuable when someone is living alone, a lifeline service or telemergency alert system that calls 911 or other emergency numbers can make everyone feel more relaxed about daily life.

New, more impressive models are being developed each year, from pendants and bracelets to phone systems—far too many to detail here. If this sort of system will make your loved one feel safer, it is a priceless choice worth researching.

Social service agencies, case workers, consultants and even groups like AARP can make recommendations, as can other residents and the staff in your loved ones' facility who may already be familiar with such aids. This is also a situation where the Internet can be extremely helpful. Search directories such as Yahoo® have a whole section devoted to medical alarms, and other search engines such as Google™ can help you find out more about the types of devices, their costs, strengths and availability.

Tip *Because of the TV advertisement that popularized the saying "I've fallen and I can't get up," the concept is often considered a standing joke. This isn't funny, though, when it happens in your family. Having a way to reach out in grim circumstances can be lifesaving as well as peace-of-mind giving.*

ⓘ Yahoo,
www.yahoo.com
ⓘ Google,
www.google.com
– search for
"personal
emergency
response
systems"

Price: up to $10
$10–$25
$26–$60

Easy if your loved one is
♥ *long distance*
♥ *local*
Delivered by retailer
Pack it yourself

Head to Heel

What's stiff and reaches both your back and your heels, and makes them both feel better?

A backscratcher and shoehorn might seem to be a funny combination at first, but this handy tool is a three-in-one bonus. Both gadgets fill useful needs for people who live alone and who don't quite have the flexibility they once enjoyed. And when you're living in a more compact space, having them combined saves just a bit of valuable room, too.

You can find this time-honored model of efficiency at general merchandise stores. We also found a version at the weather-oriented retailer Wind & Weather® for about $13.

Tip *This can be stored, with the grabber (see "Good Grabbing"), in the hot water heater closet.*

ⓘ Wind & Weather, 800-922-9463,
www.windandweather.com

Price: $10–$25

Easy if your loved one is
♥ *long distance*
♥ *local*

Delivered by retailer

Pack it yourself

Getting a Leg Up

*A*h, there's nothing like putting your feet up!

As they age and circulation becomes compromised and muscle mass decreases, people experience more leg and foot problems. Simply putting up our feet can provide a lot of relief and comfort while also being therapeutic.

A polyethylene pillow is perfect for elevating legs, whether someone is lying in bed or sitting in a favorite chair. Polyethylene and similar materials are light and easy to handle, which is important if the pillow is ever to really get used.

The shapes that work best, however, are not the ones that people are used to decorating with. Wedges, cylinders and half-circles work well, and the right size can be recommended by the staff of the shops below. You also can put a very soft terrycloth towel over the pillow so the cover doesn't have to be taken off and washed quite as often—getting that cover off can be a chore for anyone! The soft towel can go in with the regular laundry, so it's a good idea to have two.

Tip *If someone is handy with a sewing machine, the pillow cover could match the bedspread, curtains or other room fabric.*

ⓘ FootSmart®, 800-870-7149, www.footsmart.com
ⓘ Full of Life™, 800-521-7638, www.fulloflife.com
ⓘ Relax the Back®, 800-222-5728, www.relaxtheback.com

Price: $10–$25
        $61–$100

Easy if your loved one is
♥ *long distance*
♥ *local*
Delivered by retailer

In the Lap of Comfort

Many of us enjoy using a lap desk, and these compact tables are especially handy for those who are bedridden or spend a lot of time sitting in bed or a chair.

There are many types available, but my favorite comes from the retailer Brookstone. At about $80, it's a little more expensive than some, but it has a comfortable leg rest, its own light, a built-in storage area, and a cupholder.

A desk like this keeps all writing materials in one area, and it's small enough to slip next to a bed or wall. Little conveniences like this can help your loved ones keep writing longer than they might have thought they could.

Tip *A pen that is comfortable to hold (larger, fatter, grippier) makes a great addition to this gift. They run about $10.*

lab desk
- (i) Brookstone, 866-576-7337, www.brookstone.com
- (i) Silvo Home & Garden, 800-331-1261, www.silvo.com

pen
- (i) Relax the Back, 800-222-5728, www.relaxtheback.com
- (i) Isabella, 800-777-5205, www.isabellacatalog.com

lap desk
Price: $26–$60
$61–$100

Easy if your loved one is
♥ *long distance*
♥ *local*

Delivered by retailer

pen
Price: $10–$25

Easy if your loved one is
♥ *long distance*
♥ *local*

Delivered by retailer

Good Grabbing

The first time I saw the grabber in action my daughter-in-law was picking up wrapping paper after the excitement of Christmas morning gift opening. This handy tool turned out to be very useful for my mother in her care center.

It seems like an amusing device, perhaps something out of a cartoon, and yet the grabber is extraordinarily helpful. This lightweight aluminum reacher is precise enough to pick up a paper clip and strong enough "to lift a five-pound bag of sugar." This tool, which extended my mother's reach three feet, was especially helpful for making the best use of storage in both the kitchen and closets. It is also useful for reaching under the bed.

Tip *Because it's so long, the grabber is easily stored in the hot water heater closet (see "Head to Heel") or under the bed.*

ⓘ Plow and Hearth®, 800-627-1712,
www.plowandhearth.com
ⓘ Carol Wright Gifts, 402-464-6116,
www.carolwrightgifts.com

Price: up to $10
$10–$25

Easy if your loved one is
♥ *long distance*
♥ *local*
Delivered by retailer

Bonus Tip *The rubber or silicone tips of grabbers periodically need replacement. A new set is inexpensive and can usually be installed with a screwdriver. The tips, and particularly their installation, make a practical, if less than glamorous, gift. Anyone with average dexterity can perform the simple installation.*

It's For You

Having a phone that's easy to use can make a big difference for seniors, who might not call as often or talk as long on a phone that doesn't fit their needs. If vision or hand agility is an issue, a phone with big buttons can be most welcome.

Manufacturers offer many models of these phones with a variety of options. There are programmable numbers, recordable announcements, tone control, flashing ringers and Braille markings. There are even phones that call out the number as you dial! Most models feature amplified sound, too.

If you're thinking about getting this type of phone for a loved one and you have the opportunity, watch him or her use the phone a couple of times, noting any trouble hearing, handling the handset, etc. If you do buy one, before discarding the packaging, call your loved one on the new phone to ensure that its ringer tone and frequency are within his or her range of good hearing.

Tip *Consider adding a phone card as a gift, as many in this generation have grown up with reservations about using long distance.*

phones
ⓘ B Independent, 913-390-0247, www.bindependent.com
phone cards
ⓘ Costco®, 800-955-2292, www.costco.com

Price: $61–$100
            more than $100

Easy if your loved one is
♥ *long distance*
♥ *local*

Delivered by retailer

Pack it yourself

Bonus Tip *My mom didn't feel safe having her own voice on her answering machine's outgoing message. To make it sound like there was a strong male presence in the household, she requested that one of her grandsons record an appropriate greeting. Whether this was really a "comfort zone" issue or just her way of having someone else handle the confusing electronic task of getting the machine set up, we never knew. Sometimes simply supporting our loved ones is better than questioning their motives.*

Been There, Don't Do That

I learned the hard way that some things aren't at all helpful.

Here are some things you won't want to do or give:

- ❤ Although my mother loved to play cards, a card table and chairs just took up too much room for their occasional value. Most facilities have card or sitting rooms that have plenty of comfortable tables and chairs when they're needed.
- ❤ I also thought she might enjoy a big bed pillow, the kind you can wrap around you, but it turned out to be just too big and bulky, making it a nuisance during the day and little or no comfort at night. My mother appreciated the room in the bed more than a pillow she had to wrestle!
- ❤ Pets may seem like a godsend for lonely loved ones, but they can be a nightmare. Always ask first if they would like an animal, and don't even offer unless you know they can take care of them. If your loved one already has an animal, remember that special friend occasionally with a chew bone or catnip toy.

- ♥ Unless you know someone's favorite cologne, aftershave or scented bath powder, avoid giving such items as gifts. When someone loves a scent, they really love it, and when they don't, well....
- ♥ Candles can be beautiful, but they also can be quite dangerous. The number of older people lost to fires caused by candles are far greater than most of us would imagine. Fortunately, someone has come up with a wonderful alternative. The Solutions catalog has two flame-free electric candles, one that you plug in and another that runs on batteries. They're an odd-sounding idea, but their soft flicker provides a warm realistic glow. These are just right for providing a safe but beautiful addition to holiday decorating. Both turn on and off automatically and cost about $6.

Tip *It's always important for your loved ones to know that there is no need to be shy if a gift is too big or just doesn't work in their living spaces. Let your loved ones know that you want them to be comfortable saying what doesn't work as much as what does. That way you won't make a similar mistake again!*

electric candle
ⓘ Solutions®, 800-342-9988, www.solutionscatalog.com

Price: up to $10
Easy if your loved one is
- ♥ *long distance*
- ♥ *local*
Delivered by retailer

Together Time

linda Strauss Lewis

Book Club for Two

Always looking for things we could do together, I hit on the idea of having a mini-book club with my Uncle Jimmy.

We take turns choosing a book to share, giving us both opportunities to share our interests and ideas while widening our horizons. After one of us chooses the book, we both read and "discuss" them via email. This could also be done over the phone or in person. Sometimes our tastes line up well with one another, as they did when we shared *John Adams* by David McCullough.

Being the Body by Charles Colson is our current read. This back and forth is stimulating for both of us and makes for conversation beyond the weather and family news.

Tip *If your loved ones' eyesight is failing, audiobooks can make this work.*

ⓘ Amazon.com, www.amazon.com
ⓘ Barnes & Noble, 800-843-2665, www.bn.com
ⓘ Your local bookstore

Price: up to $10
  $10–$25
  $26–$60

Easy if your loved one is
♥ *long distance*
♥ *local*

Pack it yourself
Delivered by retailer

A Closer Song With Thee

As we age, our memories of the past become ever dearer. Although they sometimes cannot remember what happened yesterday, our loved ones can often recall school songs, long poems or old favorite stories.

Both my cousin Nancy and my dear friend Kay Payne began singing old hymns and camp songs to their mothers, who were in the twilight of their lives. They enjoyed singing, and their mothers found the songs soothing. Songs turned out to be an especially good distraction when uncomfortable things were occurring. The singing sessions also often drew an audience, with staff and other residents stopping to listen and appreciate this aspect of their mothers' lives.

Perhaps most delightful of all is that, even when people have stopped speaking, they sometimes will join in with the singing, transporting everyone to a happier time.

Tip *For those times we couldn't be there, we found CD's of some of my Aunt Jane's favorite music so she could sing on her own. You could even record favorite lullabies, hymns, camp songs and spirituals with family members singing along for your loved ones' pleasure.*

Price: up to $10
$10–$25

Easy if your loved one is
♥ *long distance*
♥ *local*

Pack it yourself

Bonus Tip *Try not to use songs exclusively for soothing or distraction. As singing began one day, Kay's mother said, "I know what you're doing. Something bad's going to happen!"*

Saying Our Prayers Together

Once when she was sharing her disappointment with a change at her care center, my mother gave me a fresh insight into a way to connect with her.

Part of her center's daily routine was for each resident to check in at the front desk by 9 a.m. If a resident didn't call, someone would check with him or her, first by phone and next in person. Mother had developed a pleasant relationship with the people at the front desk and looked forward to the check-in calls as a "happy start to her day."

When the care center outsourced this job to a service, she was disappointed to trade her morning contact with the happy people she knew for an interaction with unfamiliar people.

In this loss was opportunity. Even though we were far away from each other, I suggested she also call me each morning, and we could say our prayers together to start the day. She had given me the small booklet *Forward Day By Day*, which offers a short prayer for each day, as a birthday gift for many years, and I knew she subscribed, too, in the large print version. In the end, I wound up calling her every morning, and we would read that day's prayer together. Then we would say the "Our Father" together, say goodbye, and go on with the rest of our day.

I thought of the "Our Father" because, while my dad was away in the military, they would say that prayer together each evening while they were both looking at the moon. Despite sometimes many, many miles between them, they knew they were both looking at the same moon as they recited this important prayer. This extra touch of family tradition made our new custom extra special in this stage of her life.

Tip *Sometimes you'll get clues about meaningful gifts just by listening to your loved one in general conversation, especially when sharing a loss or disappointment.*

ⓘ Forward Movement Publications, 800-543-1813, www.forwardmovement.org

Price: $10–$25

Easy if your loved one is
♥ *long distance*
♥ *local*

Delivered by retailer

Getting Out and About

Visits are invaluable. Seeing loved ones in their homes is wonderful, but the opportunity for them to "escape" to other places is often priceless for them.

Yet getting out gets harder when people use wheelchairs to get around. We "got around" this challenge by purchasing a portable telescoping wheelchair ramp. Although they are a bit expensive—we paid $189 for the one we bought—they allow loved ones to visit you in your home safely, enabling them to navigate a house that may not be set up for wheelchair accessibility. The ramp also can be shared with other family members.

If accessibility is keeping you from taking wheelchair-using family members or friends outside of their facilities, a portable wheelchair ramp is well worth considering.

Tip *You can often find used equipment at secondhand stores or "gently used items" stores for more reasonable prices. Online auction sites like eBay® can also broaden your search for unusual items such as this.*

ⓘ Full of Life, 800-521-7638, www.fulloflife.com
ⓘ eBay, www.ebay.com

Price: more than $100

Easy if your loved one is
♥ *long distance*
♥ *local*

Delivered by retailer

Pack it yourself

Choice Chores

As our loved ones age, mobility becomes an issue on so many levels. Many seniors can no longer drive (or shouldn't!), and even walking can become difficult. The simplest chores begin to demand a lot more planning and skills than anyone ever realized.

Accordingly, just having someone run errands can be truly helpful. These are the kinds of things that nieces, nephews, grandchildren, and casual acquaintances can do, giving them some way to lend a hand while interacting with older loved ones.

People can:
- 💜 Go to the library to check out and return books, movies and audiobooks
- 💜 Deliver and pick up items at the dry cleaners
- 💜 Pick up favorite delicacies at the bakery
- 💜 Have jewelry repaired
- 💜 Have watch bands adjusted and batteries changed
- 💜 etc.

Tip *Shopping for clothing, undergarments and the like can be done online and sent directly to your loved one's residence.*

Easy if your loved one is 💜 *local*

Let's Be Practical

Planning to Celebrate

My Uncle Jimmy wants to be in touch with us all, but he has a hard time because he has too many things to do (mostly playing tennis, going to church and the annoyance of taking care of his ailments). So I bought a plastic accordion folder at the office supply store Staples® and made headings for each card category I thought he'd need, including:

- ♥ Birthday
- ♥ Sympathy
- ♥ Get Well
- ♥ Thinking of You
- ♥ Wedding
- ♥ Postcards
- ♥ Blank Cards
- ♥ Thank You
- ♥ Novelty

Into each slot, I placed a number of cards (the 99-Cent Discount Store made this doable). I also included a listing of birthday dates for family members, as well as some postage and return address labels. Having family members' addresses there would also be helpful.

This type of organization and having all the items in one place made it far easier for him to remember others in the family.

Tip

Consider addressing these cards for your loved one when you visit.

ⓘ Staples, 800-378-2753, www.staples.com

ⓘ For 99-Cent Discount Stores, check your local phone book

Price: $10–$25

Easy if your loved one is
- ♥ *long distance*
- ♥ *local*

Pack it yourself

A Comforting Glow

As simple as they seem, night lights can make wonderful inexpensive gifts. They are actually a good little safety aid—it's surprising how much light one can provide, making it easier to get around. Especially in the early days of living in a new, smaller place, people certainly don't need the added aggravation of stubbed toes or disconcerting feelings during the midnight search for the new bathroom.

It took some experimenting with my mother as her eyesight failed. In spite of her ability to fall asleep in a chair with the lights still on, she slept most restfully in a darkened room. Getting a night light bright enough for safety, yet dim enough for sleep, was worth the extra effort.

Night lights come in many shapes, colors, designs and motifs, so they can add a bit of personalized fun in a very small space. You can purchase one night light for each room, either getting several that match or picking out different themes for different rooms (for instance, something food-related for the kitchen). Most general merchandise stores have a variety of night lights, including ones with and without switches.

There are also fancy models that shut themselves off when it is light, such as an LED model from the Brookstone catalog. It has three settings, one that is on when motion is detected, an "always on" option, and an automatic "on at dusk, off at dawn" choice. Gump's® department store also has an elegant Gold Filigree Leaf Night Light made from a real leaf dipped in 24 karat gold. At $55, it's a very special gift.

Any of these can add a touch of joy and safety to a room.

Tip *Tune in to your loved ones' interests and give night lights that address these passions (i.e., animals, shells, etc.).*

ⓘ Brookstone, 866-576-7337, www.brookstone.com
ⓘ Gump's, 800-882-8055, www.gumps.com
ⓘ almost any department store

Price: up to $10
* $10–$25*
* $26–$60*

Easy if your loved one is
♥ *long distance*
♥ *local*

Delivered by retailer

Pack it yourself

Talking to the TV

Television brings the world inside our loved ones' homes. This is especially appreciated when they have trouble getting around. Yet sometimes even pressing remote control buttons is difficult for someone with arthritis or diminished eyesight.

Once again, technology comes to the rescue! Available through the Brookstone catalog, the InVoca™ Hands-Free Voice-Activated Remote Control lets you change channels, change volume level and even record on your VCR or DVD simply by speaking.

Tip *Most older people would need a lesson from a patient person to learn how to use this device comfortably.*

ⓘ Brookstone, 800-351-7222, www.brookstone.com

Price: $26–$60
$61–$100

Easy if your loved one is
♥ *long distance*
♥ *local*
Delivered by retailer

Rise On Up

*H*elp with some of the smallest things can make a day more pleasant. If your loved one has trouble getting up from a favorite chair, consider risers.

There are many types of risers, from small ones you slip under the feet of a chair, to pads you put on the seat, all the way up to electric seat lifts. For example, under-the-feet risers for a recliner are about $10 through Shop.com™, a 5-inch seat cushion is about $30 at the web site Comfort House®, and an Uplift Seat Assist electric system is about $190.

From my experience, the motorized risers do not move too quickly, but they can be fun for little grandkids or great grandchildren to have a "ride" on. For the little ones, having had a chance to go on Pappy's "ride" can make for special memories.

Your choice would likely be based on the kind of chair and what is easiest for your loved one, and there are many options from which to choose.

There are even risers for tables and beds, all of which can help bring comfort closer.

Tip *Putting on the risers yourself, or arranging to have it done, can be the biggest gift of all.*

ⓘ Shop.com,
www.shop.com

ⓘ Comfort House,
800-359-7701,
www.comfort
house.com

ⓘ Home Trends,
800-810-2340,
www.shophome
trends.com

ⓘ Carol Wright
Gifts,
402-464-6116,
www.carolwright
gifts.com

Price: *$10–$25*
$26–$60
$61–$100
more than $100

Easy if your loved one is
♥ *long distance*
♥ *local*

Delivered by retailer

Beautiful Baths

It was important to my mother to have a bathtub. Whenever she chose a residence, this was a consideration, because some of the studio apartments only had showers. Mother had fond memories of long luxurious baths, and now she had the time to take them. I understood this desire and didn't want to dissuade her.

As much as I wanted her to feel comfortable and in control, though, I began to worry about the bathtub and Mother's ability to get in and out of it safely. She had experienced more than one fall in the tub. Obviously, this type of accident is especially dangerous for older people, whose balance is usually waning at the same time that their bones are becoming more brittle.

Fortunately, there are several helpers available to address this concern. One is a handle that can be mounted on the side of the tub to provide leverage and stability while getting in and out.

There is also a useful safety stool that gets around the hard job of getting up and down as upper body strength declines. A safety stool can also serve the same purpose as the tub chair. The catalog company Frontgate®'s version is made to be comfortable and last a long time despite being in a wet environment, and it has rubber feet for safety, while catalog company AmeriMark®'s version is adjustable and includes a seatbelt.

Another helpful item, especially when using the stool, is a handheld shower attachment.

Mother adopted these items as they became necessary, allowing us to reach a happy medium. She was able to bathe without assistance for a long, long time by using them, and I worried less about her safety.

Tip *Even when you believe you are right, you must respect your elders' wishes as often as humanly possible. This is especially challenging when you are concerned about their safety. Look for opportunities, devices and compromises that create win/win resolutions.*

tub handle
(i) Walter Drake®, 800-525-9291, www.wdrake.com
(i) Home Trends, 800-810-2340, www.shophometrends.com
(i) Full of Life, 800-521-7638, www.fulloflife.com

safety stool/bath bench
(i) Frontgate, 800-626-6488, www.frontgate.com
(i) Walter Drake, 800-525-9291, www.wdrake.com
(i) Make Life Easier, 800-522-0227, www.make-life-easier.com
(i) The Home Marketplace, 800-356-3876, www.thehomemarketplace,com
(i) AmeriMark, 877-268-9594. www.amerimark.com

handheld shower
(i) Frontgate, 800-626-6488, www.frontgate.com
(i) Make Life Easier, 800-522-0227, www.make-life-easier.com
(i) Home Trends, 800-810-2340, www.shophometrends.com
(i) AmeriMark, 877-268-9594. www.amerimark.com

---

tub handle
Price: $26–$60

Easy if your loved one is
♥ *long distance*
♥ *local*

Delivered by retailer

safety stool/bath bench
Price: $10–$25
(Walter Drake)
  $26–$60
(Walter Drake, Make Life Easier, The Home Marketplace)
  more than $100
(Frontgate, AmeriMark)

Easy if your loved one is
♥ *long distance*
♥ *local*

Delivered by retailer

handheld shower
Price: $10–$25
  $26–$60

Easy if your loved one is
♥ *long distance*
♥ *local*

Delivered by retailer

Hair Today

Price: $10–$25

Easy if your loved one is
♥ *long distance*
♥ *local*

Delivered by retailer

For someone with arthritis, limited range of motion, or shoulder or neck pain, just combing hair can be a chore. Long-handled hairbrushes and combs can make these tasks simple again.

These brushes and combs usually have handles with good grips, and some have extensions to reach even farther. Such personal grooming aids can help a loved one continue to stay neat and clean longer, and that contributes a lot to maintaining self-esteem—no one likes to think that even the simplest tasks are beyond them.

Tip *If you're giving these as a gift to a woman, you can tie them up with pretty ribbons.*

ⓘ Accessible Environments, Inc., 800-643-5906, www.acessinc.com

The Scarves, the Wraps and the Chain Gang

In my mind's eye I usually see my mother wearing one of her lovely scarves. They were her signature item as surely as the double strand of pearls was Barbara Bush's. Throughout her life, Mother complemented and coordinated her soft outfits with attractive and appealing scarves. Of course, scarves themselves made a nice gift for her, as she was often pleased to add to her collection.

But the fun and useful item that steals the show is The Chain Gang. This plastic set of loops with attached plastic clothespins slipped easily over her closet rod and made an economical home for her light wraps and scarves. Each sliver of silk or wool had its own clip and was right there for mother to see and choose.

As her eyesight failed, it was especially helpful to have these accessories so visible, rather than packed away in a drawer. The Chain Gang (most often used to hold children's stuffed animals) also was an indispensable addition to her downsized quarters in the care center.

Tip *When coming up with gifts for your loved ones, don't be afraid to suggest alternative uses for everyday items. Try this while shopping at stores with a focus on children or young people.*

ⓘ Organize.com, 800-600-9817, www.organize-everything.com

ⓘ Pallets, 866-543-3325 x22, www.kidssurplus.com

Price: up to $10

Easy if your loved one is
❤ *long distance*
❤ *local*

Delivered by retailer

Get a Grip

Good handles make life a lot easier for people who don't have the grip or dexterity they might once have had.

Fat-handled peelers, knives, spatulas and other kitchen utensils may take up a little more room in the drawer, but they are worth it for anyone who has challenges handling smaller items. You can find these utensils and many others in kitchen shops, general merchandise stores and, of course, online. OXO® offers an entire line of easy-to-handle utensils called GoodGrips® that is widely available. We also found a good selection of grip-friendly gear at Life Solutions Plus®.

Other items we use everyday can provide similar challenges. Round doorknobs and lamps can be made easier to open and turn on with the addition of levers and easy-grip knobs. Such simple helpers are inexpensive but worth more than their weight and cost in convenience and ability extension.

Door handle grippers usually slip over an existing knob, providing a slip-free surface. They're great for anyone with limited hand strength. The Wright Stuff even has one that glows in the dark for about $6.

Easy-to-turn lamp knobs can replace the old switch. Hand Helpers offers a large, three-spoked version that provides more leverage and fits most standard lamps for about $7.

Elder Store offers a few types of lamp knobs, as well as an extender for light switches that's handy for people who are in wheelchairs.

These are all small issues, but they're the sort of little things that make life easier, and we all know every little bit helps!

Tip *Installing these items while you are visiting makes it more likely they will get out of the box.*

big handled utensils
- (i) Life Solutions Plus, 877-785-8326, www.lifesolutionsplus.com
- (i) The Wright Stuff, 877-750-0376, www.wrightstuff.biz
- (i) Most kitchen stores

door knobs and lamp handles
- (i) The Wright Stuff, 877-750-0376, www.wrightstuff.biz
- (i) Hand Helpers, 888-632-7091, www.handhelpers.com
- (i) Elder Store, 888-833-8875, www.elderstore.com

big handled utensils
Price: *up to $10*
$10–$25
$26–$60

Easy if your loved one is
♥ *long distance*
♥ *local*

Delivered by retailer

Pack it yourself

door knobs and lamp handles
Price: *up to $10*

Easy if your loved one is
♥ *long distance*
♥ *local*

Delivered by retailer

Pack it yourself

Golden Gadgets

*T*here are a number of organizations and companies that focus on serving the elderly. One of my favorites is Gold Violin®, which offers "gadgets for independent living."

Gold Violin has an awesome collection of canes, as well as extra large playing cards, dominoes, dice, crossword puzzles, address books, check registers, calendars and even large print computer keyboard labels.

This is a great source for practical gifts, and your loved one may also want to be able to order items directly.

Tip *If you order a catalog for yourself as well as your loved one, you may look through it together and discuss things in person or over the phone.*

ⓘ Gold Violin, 877-648-8400, www.goldviolin.com

Price: up to $10
$10–$25
$26–$60

Easy if your loved one is
♥ *long distance*
♥ *local*

Delivered by retailer

Just the Ticket

What can fit in an envelope, yet transport your loved ones to places of joy, nostalgia and fun?

Tickets of all kinds are thoughtful gifts that show you are really thinking of them. For instance, for a loved one who loves to sew, consider tickets to a fabric show or a play like "The Quiltmaker's Gift."

If you live in town, include tickets for yourself, as this is a great activity you can do together. If you live out of town, you can include a ticket for a friend in their facility.

Tickets to sporting events, movies, the ballet, ice show and theatre are all wonderful. "Big ticket" trips to visit friends or family by airplane or bus, or a cruise to a long-dreamed-about foreign land are all welcome and thoughtful for those who can travel. Even lottery tickets can be a great and inexpensive gift that add a little excitement to brighten someone's day.

Tip *My friend Christine Hughes liked to deliver her tickets inside of a helium balloon to add pizzazz.*

ⓘ Ticketmaster®, www.ticketmaster.com

Price: up to $10
   $10–$25
   $26–$60
   $61–$100
   more than $100

Easy if your loved one is
♥ *long distance*
♥ *local*

Delivered by retailer
Pack it yourself

Warm as Toast

A sandwich is a staple for easy and nutritious food, yet they may seem routine and ordinary to your loved one. Warming that sandwich or snack adds pizzazz.

It's easy to make grilled cheese sandwiches, warm turnovers, wraps, cheese rolls and other delectable goodies with an ingenious little English product called Toastabags. They let you use an ordinary toaster or toaster oven to make what would otherwise be a gooey mess without the Toastabags.

You just pop what you want warmed in one of these reusable bags, slip it into the toaster, and, once it's done, slide it onto a plate. It's a simple, easy, clean and convenient way to make a warm snack.

Tip *Recipes are included, increasing the value of the toaster bags.*

(i) Toastabags, 44-0-1684 574797, www.toastabags.com

Price: up to $10

Easy if your loved one is
♥ *long distance*
♥ *local*

Delivered by retailer

Gifts
of
Fancy

Tiny Vases Full of Love

Delightful small pitchers were my mother's passion, and she accumulated quite a collection. As I grew up, she set a lovely table for supper that always included one of her pitchers and a tiny bouquet or even a single flower.

This tradition was an opening into a way to grace her room in the care center. I purchased a tiny glass vase that dropped into a brass ring that attached to the wall. Then I asked the staff at the care center front desk to find the florist that most often delivered to the facility.

My next stop was at the recommended flower shop. I was actually able to show the florist the vase, and we worked out an arrangement. Each and every time she delivered to anyone at the center for any reason, the florist would bring along a tiny bouquet or single flower to my mother's apartment.

Saving the delivery charge, the cost for the flowers was modest, and was simply charged to my credit card. My mother was surprised and delighted by the flowers and, even as her sight faded, she continued to enjoy their fragrance.

Tip *Being able to show the florist the vase made it easy for her to know how many flowers it would hold.*

Price: up to $10
$10–$25

Perishable

Easy if your loved one is ♥ *long distance*

Delivered by retailer

Sweet Scents

Some people say that the strongest memories are those associated with smells. Yet odors are sometimes so subtle we often forget their value.

In addition to its scents, potpourri makes a nice gift for a woman because it looks nice, is inexpensive and easy to mail. It's also an especially good choice for a nursing home setting, as anything that helps the room smell nice and gives it distinction is appreciated.

I send potpourri to my Aunt Jane at Thanksgiving, and there are also often special mixes for spring, summer and Christmas. I buy a large bagful, with pods, berries and other interesting contents, for about $18 at our nearby Hallmark shop, and you can also order it on their web site. Touchstone catalog also has some lovely Gardener's Delight Potpourri with a gardenia scent.

Tip *The bagful fits nicely into a wicker basket I bought just for this purpose at a garage sale for $1. We use the basket over and over again, to bring sweet smells...and maybe a pleasant memory or two.*

(i) Hallmark, www.hallmark.com
(i) Touchstone, 800-962-6890, www.touchstonecatalog.com

Price: $10–$25

Easy if your loved one is
♥ *long distance*
♥ *local*

Delivered by retailer

Pack it yourself

Delicious Delicacies

*T*here are many services that deliver favorite foods, either upon request or on a scheduled basis, whether it's monthly, every other month or quarterly.

While food purveyor Harry and David® is famous for its pears, its Granny Smith apples dipped in silky caramel and delectable milk chocolate are irresistible for many of us. They have all sorts of gifts, though, from healthy fruits to towers of candy. They'd love to send you a catalog, if you don't already get one.

Food treats are often a good way to get our loved ones to eat, as many of them lose their appetites as they age. Although sweets aren't always the best choice, when someone reaches their golden years, why deny them pleasure? And who cares about calories!

Tip *See's Candies® sends delicious treats and even has candy with no sugar.*

ⓘ Harry and David, 877-322-1200, www.harryanddavid.com
ⓘ See's Candies, 800-347-7337, www.seescandies.com

Price: $26–$60

Consumable

Perishable

Easy if your loved one is
♥ *long distance*
♥ *local*

Delivered by retailer

Pack it yourself

Bonus Tip *Cutting the apples into quarters makes them easier to eat.*

Some other sources:

- ⓘ Birthday Cake to Go, 877-846-6404, www.birthdaycaketogo.com
- ⓘ Bissinger's®, 800-325-8881, www.bissingers.com
- ⓘ Cakework, 415-821-1333, www.cakework.com
- ⓘ Dean & DeLuca, 800-221-7714, www.deandeluca.com
- ⓘ Delightful Deliveries, 800-708-0024, www.delightfuldeliveries.com
- ⓘ Junior's Cheesecakes, 800-958-6467, www.juniorscheesecake.com
- ⓘ Tortuga Rum Cakes, 877-486-7884, www.tortugarums.com
- ⓘ Very Vera, 800-500-8372, www.veryvera.com
- ⓘ Williams-Sonoma®, 877-812-6235, www.williams-sonoma.com
- ⓘ Williamsburg®, 800-446-9240, www.williamsburgmarketplace.com

Finest Find

Price: more than $100

Consumable

Perishable

Easy if your loved one is
♥ *long distance*
♥ *local*

Delivered by retailer

My hands-down favorite item in this book is a perfect delight: it's easy for the sender, healthy and delicious for the recipient, a great conversation starter and gives cachet to your loved one.

My son, Brad, and his wife, Lisa, sent this gift to my mother and it was a blessing: The Harry and David catalog has a Light Size Fruit of the Month Club®. Each month, a delicious offering of apples, nectarine, pears and other selections arrive for your loved one. It is just the right size: not overwhelming, but with enough to share with a friend or neighbor. The fruit is so beautiful and tasty that it makes the perfect thoughtful gift to share. One peach from this bounty is an easy way to get people chatting.

Tip *Keep your eyes open for gifts that can be shared within the care center or apartment complex. It is very good for your loved one's esteem to have a treat to share. The comment, "My grandson sent these," goes a long way, too.*

ⓘ Harry and David, 877-322-1200, www.harryanddavid.com

It's in the Mail

*T*hanks to the Internet, there are many services that are now available by mail.

We all know that books can be ordered online and delivered to your loved one's door, but there are also rental services, which keep down the clutter.

For example, audiobooks can be rented online. They often come with a prepaid return mailer that lets your loved one or a caregiver simply slip the tape back into the box and stick it in the mail.

Movies can be rented, too. Again, you can select the movies on the Internet, then have them mailed directly to your family member or friend, along with a prepaid return envelope. Netflix offers a wonderful service for less than $20 a month that lets you choose movies in advance. It allows participants to have as many as three movies in their possession at a time, and they can keep the movies for however long they wish, with no late fees. As they return the movies in their prepaid envelopes, their next choices are automatically delivered.

Your library may also have the option to mail back books, movies and audiobooks. Contact the library directly for more information about its services.

Tip *Your loved one's care facility may have an Internet station in its library, giving you something to do together during a visit. You can sit at the monitor and go through the possibilities. Or you can print out lists of choices in advance and bring them with your during a visit, using the paper version to help your loved one pick out what he or she wants without having to involve too much technology.*

(i) Amazon.com, www.amazon.com
(i) Barnes & Noble, 800-843-2665, www.bn.com
(i) Your local bookstore
(i) NetFlix, www.netflix.com

Price: $10–$25

Easy if your loved one is
♥ *long distance*
♥ *local*

Delivered by retailer

Flaunting Flowers

A corsage is a gift of love, whether it's for a prom or just for fun. That led me to buy my mother wrist corsages that she could wear around the care center. The best part of this inexpensive gift is that it keeps your loved one in the spotlight for the day she wears it.

First, everyone who comes in contact with her will have a chance to ask about the corsage and its significance. Getting to tell the story of a son or daughter sending the flower gives everyone something new and positive to talk about. This is one of the ways even a shy or modest loved one can be fussed over gently and appropriately. Second, it is always in her field of vision and even provides some fragrance.

Third, this gift is easy for everyone. It means no extra flowers or plants for your loved one or the staff to attend to, including finding a place in the room to put an arrangement, watering or other care. And no one in this age group needs the bother of pins to attach the flower to clothing.

My mother loved carnations and their spicy smell. If you are aware of your loved ones' favorite flower, this is something to share with his or her local florist when placing your order.

Tip *If you're not in the same town as your loved one, it's wise to have a phone book for his or her town. You can also use the Internet to find a local shop, although sites such as Dex® at www.dexonline.com and Switchboard® at www.switchboard.com aren't always as complete or accurate as a hometown phone book. Sending flowers locally is much less expensive when FTD charges are not involved. You can also use the Internet to send a corsage from a place such as Amy's Plantrex Flower Shop.*

ⓘ Amy's Plantrex Flower Shop, 877-526-8739,
   www.plantrex.com

Price: $26–$60

Perishable

Easy if your loved one is
♥ *long distance*
♥ *local*

Delivered by retailer

The Magic of Lights

My Aunt Jane's eyesight has greatly diminished due to macular degeneration. While I was visiting this amazing woman one January, she gave me a clue for a special gift for her.

While she and I sat on the couch, held hands, and visited, her caretaker took it upon herself to take down the Christmas tree and decorations in a nearby room. This gesture, meant to be helpful, upset Aunt Jane. She cried out, "I loved the lights because I could see them out of my peripheral vision. They cast a magic spell."

Having heard this remark, I was delighted to find a set of fiber optic butterflies that created a light show. This gift was easily sent to Aunt Jane's care center by way of a catalogue and 800 number. The center staff was puzzled by them, however, and put the lights away in a box.

I gave my dear cousin Pat a "heads up" about the butterflies. To Aunt Jane's delight, Pat found them and put them up.

The win here for me was the sense of having gotten something for her that replaced something she was missing. So many of the things our loved ones pine for cannot be replaced. I was pleased when Pat told me how pretty they look and how happy my aunt was to have the magic of lights in her room once again.

Tip *Just sending the gift isn't always enough. If you live far away, make sure it actually gets put to use (as long as your loved one really wants it!). Sometimes, as in this case, the caregivers just didn't understand the purpose of the gift. A nice note or phone call can make the difference, while further strengthening your relationship with them. It also subtly communicates how much you care about your loved one, which can help them hold that person in higher regard.*

(i) Collections Etc.™, 620-584-8000,
www.collectionsetc.com

Price: $10–$25

Easy if your loved one is
♥ *long distance*
♥ *local*

Pack it yourself

Any Holiday Is a Good Holiday

While birthdays and other major holidays often call for a gift or visit, My Aunt Jane and I celebrated *everything*.

It doesn't have to be expensive. In February, I sent her colorful Mardi Gras beads I'd bought at Hallmark for $2. At Jo-Ann^{SM}, the fabric and craft shop, I found a shamrock pin for St. Patrick's Day and a Valentine heart for Aunt Jane's blouse. Caspari® also makes cute paper hankies for all holidays that usually cost about $1.50 and fit nicely into greeting cards. You can often find these paper tissues at some store checkout counters.

Hallmark, which also sells cute pins that can be worn on a lapel or collar to signify the season or the day, has, of course, a splendid collection of appropriate cards. Sometimes they sell packages of holiday cards at discounted prices—for example, 8 Halloween cards with envelopes.

When sending one of the cards to your loved one, with the tissues or pin included, consider sending the other 7 cards already addressed and stamped. Older people often lose the wherewithal to do thoughtful things like sending cards to important people in their lives, so this gives them a head start (for other ideas in this vein, see "Planning to Celebrate"). In this scenario, all they have to do is sign their name.

Keeping these celebrations low cost lets you both enjoy lots of holidays—you can even make up some, if you want. For more fun holidays, see "Holidays" at the back of this book, or try the book *Celebrate Today* by John Kremer.

Tip *Look for items that will slip into a greeting card envelope (beads, pins, hankies, etc.) to simplify mailing.*

ⓘ Hallmark, www.hallmark.com
ⓘ Jo-Ann, www.joanns.com has a store locator
ⓘ Amazon.com, www.amazon.com
ⓘ Barnes & Noble, 800-843-2665, www.bn.com

Price: up to $10
$10–$25

Easy if your loved one is
♥ *long distance*
♥ *local*

Pack it yourself

Ribbons and Bows

*I*n looking for ways to add decorative touches to my mother's studio apartment without taking up valuable space, I came upon the lovely new fanciful ribbons that are on the market.

For example, I added a ribbon to a small gift book, wrapping it much like a present, and got a lot of effect for no more room and very little money. These ribbons can be added to pillows, used to hang keys on a key rack, or tied to items like the small pitchers Mother collected. She seemed delighted, often asking, "What did you do to that little book? It looks lovely!"

I first found these delightful items at the Calico Corners fabric and trim shop near my home in Arizona. I was drawn to their seemingly endless colors, patterns, fabrics, widths and textures.

Search for a Calico Corners near you at their web site, or there may be other fabric or craft stores nearby that carry these beautiful ribbons.

Tip *There also is a book on the market for dozens of ideas about the many creative uses of ribbons called* Ribbons: Beautiful Ideas for Gifts and Home Decorations *by Mary Norden and Sandra Lane. It's available at the online bookstores as well as many local shops.*

ⓘ Calico Corners, 800-213-6366, www.calico corners.com

ⓘ Amazon.com, www.amazon.com

ⓘ Barnes & Noble, 800-843-2665, www.bn.com

Price: up to $10

Easy if your loved one is
❤ *long distance*
❤ *local*

Pack it yourself

Soft & Snuggly

All Things Cashmere

My mother lived graciously, but always on a budget. Once when we were visiting, she told me that, if life had been otherwise, she would have liked to wear cashmere and give it as gifts.

This led to me splurging for a once-in-a-lifetime gift that was completely out of our normal price range. Yet a full-length, all-cashmere bathrobe was a luxury item that brought hours of pleasure. She told me once that she believed the robe had saved her life: as her circulation slowed down, she was sensitive to cold weather and drafts. It was evident that this bathrobe was a treasured gift and that filled my heart with delight.

Mother so loved the cashmere robe that I looked for other things made of this remarkably soft wool. Socks became another favorite cashmere "luxury"—at $38 they were a real bargain, compared to the cashmere robe. It was worth it, considering the great pleasure she got from cashmere.

She also enjoyed cashmere gloves and anything made of tissue-thin pashmina cashmere. Pashmina, which comes from the fine undergrowth of wool of the Chyangra mountain goat of the Himalayas, seems to get softer with each use. It can be folded into nearly nothing and slipped into a purse or pocket. Many older people chill easily, so compact, soft and warm wool can be a blessing in so many ways. Nordstrom's carries a particularly light wrap for $99.

It is best to wash anything made of this wool by hand in Woolite®. This wasn't a big problem for my mother, who was famous for washing things by hand.

At the very end of her life, however, we gave her the gift of someone to do her laundry. Even though they did laundry at the care center, her skin was very sensitive and their harsh detergent and extra hot water made her bedding, towels and clothing uncomfortable. Having someone wash her things a little more gently was just a little something we could do to make her daily life better. (Thank you, Essie.)

Tip *When you select an item, think about how much care it will require and who will do it.*

- ⓘ Nordstrom, 888-282-6060, www.nordstrom.com
- ⓘ Soft Surroundings®, 800-240-7076, www.softsurroundings.com
- ⓘ Schweitzer Linen, 800-554-6367, www.schweitzerlinen.com
- ⓘ Frontgate, 800-626-6488, www.frontgate.com

Price: $26–$60
$61–$100

Delivered by retailer

Sock (and Shoe) It to Me

There are a number of products that can help people with limited strength and mobility put on stockings and socks. One popular tool is a donner, which helps with stockings—it's especially appreciated with support stockings, which can require strength to pull on.

Sock aids are a simple cloth or plastic device with long cloth or cord handles that help in pulling on socks or stockings. They usually cost less than $20.

The socks are on, but now what about the shoes? Tying laces requires dexterity and leaning, which is why slip-ons become popular for older people. But if your loved one has a favorite pair of shoes or falls in love with a new pair that requires laces, consider elastic shoe laces or coilers, such as those at AmeriMark.

Coilers, which look like a slender cloth Slinky, are popular with younger people, too, so you can sometimes find them in bright colors and fun patterns. Both the elastic and coiler versions let you tie the shoes once, then slip them on thereafter. At $2–4, they're enough to make you *look* for lace-ups!

Tip *The right shoes and socks are a health and safety issue as well as a matter of comfort and ease.*

ⓘ AmeriMark,
877-268-9594,
www.amerimark.
com

ⓘ Home Trends,
800-810-2340,
www.shophome
trends.com

ⓘ Walter Drake,
800-525-9291,
www.wdrake.com

🗝

Price: up to $10
$10–$25

Easy if your loved one is
♥ *long distance*
♥ *local*
Delivered by retailer

So Soft

There's nothing like slipping between soft sheets for a good night's rest. For people with sensitive skin, it's almost a necessity.

The best bedding is 100% Egyptian, long-combed cotton. My uncle, who has skin problems, always appreciates cotton sheets and pillowcases as a gift. I keep my eye out for sales and am ready when an occasion such as his birthday arises. He would rather have the best cotton than a matching set. But then, he is a bachelor.

Tip *Almost all stores carry sheets with high thread count these days, but it is the long-combed cotton that makes the difference.*

ⓘ Vermont Country Store®, 802-362-8460, www.vermontcountrystore.com

Price: *$10–$25*
$26–$60

Easy if your loved one is
♥ *long distance*
♥ *local*

Delivered by retailer

Cuddle Up

Running hot and cold can actually be a benefit when it comes to those aches and pains that come with age. And this is one modern solution that has nothing to do with technology.

You can now buy small buckwheat pillows with soft, decorative coverings. They can be heated in a microwave to relieve tension, anxiety, stiff and sore muscles, aching joints, cramps, migraines, backaches, arthritis pain, toothaches and earaches, or just to warm cold feet on a chilly winter night.

This same little pillow can be chilled in a freezer to sooth sore muscles, ease joint pain, insect bites, sinus pain, hot flashes and reduce inflammation or swelling.

Tip *Bucky also makes a great neckwrap.*

ⓘ Bucky® Products, Inc., 800-692-8259, www.bucky.com

Price: $26–$60

Easy if your loved one is
- ❤ *long distance*
- ❤ *local*

Delivered by retailer

Snuggle Right

In almost every part of the world, there are times a nice wool blanket is perfect for a good night's sleep. Other times, a light covering is preferable.

That's why each person at my aunt's nursing home has both a wool, or wool-like, blanket and a cotton quilt at the end of the bed. These blankets and quilts were supplied by family and friends, so they often reflected the residents through their various colors and patterns, thereby also providing some individuality, which is always at a premium in these facilities.

They were most often used at night, but these spreads also came in handy when residents sat in a chair and wanted something over their knees or lap while reading or visiting.

Tip *Washability is important to the usefulness of these covers.*

ⓘ Soft Surroundings, 800-240-7076,
www.softsurroundings.com

Price: *$10–$25*
$26–$60

Easy if your loved one is
♥ *long distance*
♥ *local*

Delivered by retailer

Pack it yourself

The Sweet Smell of Dignity

Price: up to $10

Easy if your loved one is
♥ long distance
♥ local

Pack it yourself

Nursing homes usually provide the products used for caring for your loved ones. That doesn't mean, though, that there aren't other supplies that might be better.

Once when visiting my aunt, I had a helpful conversation with the aide who bathed her. She let us in on a professional secret: Dove® soap and Gold Bond® Powder, both of which are easily available at most drugstores, handle unpleasant odors well. This is especially helpful when a loved one has begun using disposable undergarments.

The aide also advised us to write my aunt's name on each of these "upgraded" items that we brought in. She explained that the good stuff would quickly be used up by other staff members as the first choices for their patients if ownership were not clearly indicated.

If the care facility doesn't already use these products, they are worth the small extra cost for the comfort and dignity.

Tip *Hands-on caregivers such as aides are often wonderful resources for truly helpful information and tips.*

ⓘ most drugstores

Silent Night

If you've lived in a home for decades, you get used to its sights and sounds: the soft glow of a streetlight, the creak of steps, the hiss of radiators, wind in nearby trees.

When people move into an assisted living center or even an apartment or condo, more distractions come along with it, especially the lights and sounds of other people who live closer than they had been used to. An unexpected casualty can be a good night's deep sleep. That makes anything that helps quiet the night attractive.

Eye shades can help by blocking out light while feeling cool and soft against the skin. You can use something as simple as a cloth hair band, or there's now also a new twist on the time-honored version, a foam filled mask that also contains a four-track sound system. One you can find at Hammacher Schlemmer[SM] offers the soothing sounds of nature, such as ocean waves, rain forest, rippling brook and raindrops. It has a volume control and runs on three AAA batteries.

If your loved one doesn't want eyeshades, there are other ways to silence unwanted sound. Appliances such as the Sleep Sound Generator and Sound Oasis we found at Hammacher Schlemmer make simple sounds that block annoying noises such as traffic or loud clocks. Even with adjustable levels and tones, these devices cost about $50 or $60.

My aunt has a roommate who has to have the TV volume up high in order to hear it, so this enabled them each to find mutual peace.

Tip *Another option is a noise-cancelling cordless headset sold by Radio Shack®, Bose® and other companies, that lets the person who needs the louder TV or radio to control the volume without disturbing others. Prices begin at about $30.*

ⓘ eTravelerGear, 401-615-2862, www.etravelergear.com
ⓘ Hammacher Schlemmer, 800-321-1484,
   www.hammacherschlemmer.com
ⓘ Radio Shack, 800-843-7422, www.radioshack.com
ⓘ Bose, 800-999-2673, www.bose.com
ⓘ Full of Life, 800-521-7638, www.fulloflife.com

Price: $26–$60

Easy if your loved one is
♥ *long distance*
♥ *local*

Delivered by retailer

Making Much of Memories

Picturing the Past

Memories are truly precious to aging people—I'm aware of this as I myself grow older. And as memories begin to fade, scrapbooks can be extremely useful. Too, as our loved ones move into smaller quarters, they often must part with many things that carry fond memories or even real usefulness.

Not all scrapbooks are the same, however. There are useful types for our loved ones themselves, and another type for other people *about* them.

The first type was made by my friend Kay Payne for her mother and dad as they moved into a care center. Kay made a scrapbook of their home of many years, with many pictures of the house inside and out, as well as of their beloved possessions. After all, photos of beloved belongings *can* go along to their new homes. Memory books with pictures of favorite artwork, a longtime lounge chair, even an old pair of tennis shoes with holes worn lovingly in them can still be part of their lives in a memory book.

Kay also took pictures of her parents' moving day, starting at their longtime home and then following through as they moved into their new quarters in the care center. This history provided a sense of grounding as well as excitement for the couple as they cherished memories of their old home and adjusted to their new one. After all, we only chronicle worthy events!

All it takes is a little time to photograph items and places before a household is dismantled. The pictures can be sorted and pasted in a book later—in fact, this makes a good "together time" activity.

The second type of scrapbook was made by my cousin Nancy for her mother, my Aunt Jane. It was really as much for other people as for Aunt Jane. Nancy named it *Things You Need to Know About Jane Schutt*. She made a collection of facts and pictures that gave any of the staff who would come into contact with her mother a sense of who she is and was. Aunt Jane is losing much of her memory, and this book makes it easier for the staff to interact with her, as well as to understand that she is a person worthy of respect and care. The book also gives them a head start in knowing what things to talk about with her. This is much easier than simply asking questions of Aunt Jane, especially since she responds much better to conversations about important people and times in her own life.

Both of these women expressed their caring in such a personal and special way through these captured memories, giving them a way to show their love and appreciation of their parents.

Tip *Knowing what to talk about with people who are losing their memory can be challenging. Sharing such scrapbooks is a wonderful place to start conversations when visiting.*

ⓘ Aaron Brothers®, 888-372-6464, www.aaron brothers.com

ⓘ Michaels®, 800-642-4235, www.michaels. com

🔑

Price: $10–$25
$26–$60

Easy if your loved one is
♥ *long distance*
♥ *local*

Pack it yourself

Pictures Worth a Thousand Laughs

Sometimes I send my uncle things to throw away. No, I'm not encouraging him (or myself) to be wasteful. It's just that sometimes it's the *idea* that counts.

Take, for example, the green top hat I bought him for St. Patrick's Day. It was inexpensive and was pretty much only good one day of the year. The hat also took up a fair amount of room for someone who doesn't have much space to spare in his living quarters.

And that's where the *idea* comes in. My uncle was to wear the silly *chapeau*—or have friends wear it—and then have someone take some photos of him and his friends. Once the pictures were taken, the hat would be expendable. The photos and the fun, however, will last a long, long time.

Among the other things I've sent for these silly-making occasions are three amazing masks I found in a catalog. The paper faces were easy to send, and my uncle and his pals had hours of fun swapping the masks and taking pictures of each other wearing them, sometimes in goofy poses. The photos went right up on his bulletin board. The masks? They have probably gone on to some deserving recycling bin.

Tip *Sometimes it helps to include a note that your loved one should enjoy the photo-taking and then throw away the item. Such a message can give permission to someone who is likely from a generation of savers to toss the props.*

Price: up to $10
* $10–$25*

Easy if your loved one is
♥ *long distance*
♥ *local*
Delivered by retailer
Pack it yourself

The Happiest Calendar of Them All

Price: $10–$25

Easy if your loved one is
- ♥ *long distance*
- ♥ *local*

Pack it yourself

Items that reminded Mother of friends and family were special to her, and one of her most cherished gifts of all time was a simple calendar my brother and his family made for her one year.

They took 12 family photos to their local Kinko's copy shop, which has a service that makes it especially easy to make a calendar. Each month revealed new photos of this handsome and fun family, bringing back countless memories for my mother.

Clearly she enjoyed and savored the thoughtful gift during the year for which it was given and beyond. Even as her eyesight faded, she kept this calendar close by. It was near her Bible, her large-print dictionary and her poetry of Robert Frost. I found it in her treasured things after her death. The dates had long since lost their currency, but the photos of her children, grandchildren and her pal "Beau," the dog, were still as dear to her as the first time she saw them.

Tip *Instead of writing the names of the people on the days of their birthdays, consider pasting photos of their faces onto their special day. Pasting the pictures on is something you can also do together.*

ⓘ FedEx Kinko's, 800-463-3339, www.kinkos.com

Quilted Chronicles

Wall space often becomes treasured territory when living in a small apartment or room. It can quickly become filled with photos, calendars, mirrors and other trimmings that make the place homey.

Fortunately, there are other places that can be personalized with precious memories. One such highly visible location is the bed, where a handmade quilt can become a source of great joy—and casual conversation, something that is also quite prized in care facilities.

Sometimes family members come together, each donating a square that features something dear to the person. My cousin Pat Herzog appliquéd quotations from her mother's own journal, using freezer paper to transfer the words to the material. Another used transfers she printed from her own computer to apply photographs to the cloth. Yet another simply sewed flowers and butterflies, as her mother loved both.

If the quilt becomes a family project, you may want to recommend a technique (photos, patchwork, etc.) or a theme ("through the generations," "words of wisdom," etc.) for that particular spread.

Such a quilt provides hours of priceless pleasure and memories.

Tip

The photo transfers are easier than they might first appear. Transfer sheets, such as those made by Avery, are available at most computer supply outlets. It's amazing what you can do with an inkjet printer and a warm iron!

ⓘ Avery®, 800-462-8379, www.avery.com

ⓘ Avery products are also sold at most office supply stores

⚷

Price: $10–$25

Easy if your loved one is
♥ *long distance*
♥ *local*

Pack it yourself

Dynamic Display

A bulletin board is perfect for posting photos, postcards and greeting cards, and a "French bulletin board" is especially practical when you don't want to fuss with thumbtacks. Rather than cork, a French bulletin board has a cloth backing with stretchy, ribbon-like bands across it. You can simply tuck the corners or tops and bottoms of cards and photos under the bands. This makes it easy to display things, even for people whose hands aren't quite as cooperative as they once were when handling small items such as tacks.

If you can't find a French bulletin board, even a regular one will work. Or you can make your own French version by stapling elastic ribbons across an existing bulletin or cloth-covered board.

Regardless, just having a place to put daily reminders of the people and places in your life is a wonderful way to make a room or apartment more homey.

Tip *Friends and family who often wonder what they can do for a loved one may wish to decorate the board, giving it a colorful border or adding holiday images at appropriate times of the year. Craft shops such as Michaels have decorative paper and fabric, as well as shamrocks, Easter bunnies, Thanksgiving turkeys and other holiday materials to dress up a board.*

ⓘ Michaels, 800-642-4235, www.michaels.com

Price: $10–$25
  $26–$60

Easy if your loved one is
♥ *long distance*
♥ *local*
Delivered by retailer
Pack it yourself

Seeing Stories

When everyone lives in similar rooms along similar hallways, it's easy to forget that they once had their own homes and their own lives.

Moving into an assisted living facility or nursing home means "rebinding" your life story—as much as we want to see people as individuals, it's difficult when their needs become as similar as their surroundings.

In addition to a memory scrapbook (see "Picturing the Past"), I found that photographs posted in a loved one's living place helped people remember that they had once had vital and often interesting lives. The way I learned this, however, was by being reminded myself.

After she had moved to a nursing home, my Aunt Jane had a roommate. Above her roommate's bed, in simple but attractive paper mats, were 8 x 10" photographs of her in happier days. Seeing those pictures reminded me that she had once been an active person and helped me relate to her more respectfully. I was grateful for the daily reminder, and put similar photos above my aunt's bed.

Sometimes photos of other family members are helpful in keeping family close. Although space for pictures is at a premium, there are several solutions, ranging from the ordinary to high tech.

An ordinary idea is magnetic frames for the refrigerator. Uncle Jimmy reports that he feels a lift as he goes out to his kitchen and sees our photos smiling at him.

A leather bookmark with a space for a picture at the top takes no room and is great for your loved ones who like to read. If you cut out a paper template the size of the bookmark's photo and keep it for yourself, you can send along an update and be sure it will fit. I simply traced the size on a piece of paper that I use as a placeholder in whatever book I use regularly.

A high-tech version is a digital photo frame that holds and displays 80 pictures one after another automatically. It costs about $150 at Best Buy®.

Tip *Give your loved ones permission to throw away old pictures when you replace them with updated ones. The last thing they usually need is something else to store, but in times past, you just didn't throw things away. If a photo is a true treasure, they will keep it against your advice, but having your encouragement to toss them may help.*

framing mats
ⓘ Aaron Brothers, 888-372-6464, www.aaronbrothers.com
ⓘ Michaels, 800-642-4235, www.michaels.com

leather bookmark
ⓘ Solutions, 800-342-9988, www.solutionscatalog.com

digital photo frame
ⓘ Best Buy, www.bestbuy.com

framing mats
Price: up to $10
        $10–$25

Easy if your loved one is
♥ *long distance*
♥ *local*

Delivered by retailer
Pack it yourself

leather bookmark
Price: up to $10

Easy if your loved one is
♥ *long distance*
♥ *local*

Delivered by retailer

digital photo frame
Price: more than $100

Pack it yourself
Delivered by retailer

The Silver Box

My sister-in-law, Mary Margaret, created a gift of encouragement for my mother designed from the book *Silver Boxes* by Florence Littauer.

Using the recommendations from this wonderful book, she bought a 4" x 3" silver plated box. (We also found a really nice heart-shaped one at Bliss!™'s BlissWeddingsMarket.com.) She asked all of our family members to write special memories of my mother and send them directly to her rather than Mother, keeping all of this a surprise.

Mary Margaret then took each recollection and typed it neatly. She cut them out into small slips and rolled them into scrolls, and filled the box with these intriguing twirls. At a special dinner, the scrolls were unrolled and read to my mother. She also had the box as a keepsake of this special time.

Tip *To each of his memories, my son Brad added the four words, "and I felt loved." In reading his memories, this phrase brought tears to Mother's eyes every time.*

ⓘ BlissWeddingsMarket.com, 866-445-4405,
www.blissweddingsmarket.com

Price: $10–$25

Easy if your loved one is
❤ *long distance*
❤ *local*

Pack it yourself

What Is Love?

How do you like to be loved? Surprisingly, many of us have different preferences for how people can best show us they care.

A book that might be helpful is *The Five Love Languages* by Dr. Gary Chapman. It identifies the five basic ways most people like to be loved:

1. Words of affirmation
2. Receiving gifts
3. Quality time
4. Acts of service
5. Physical touch

Each of these can prompt further realization of what your loved ones prefer, whether it's a regular phone call, handwritten letters, a hug or the simple yet powerful words "I love you."

Your loved ones could read this book and you could discuss what they discover, or you could read the book together, giving you the activity and time together *and* some valuable insights.

Tip *Whatever way you approach it, one big benefit will be better understanding what moves your loved one most, so you can "hit the bull's-eye" more often by doing what means the most.*

ⓘ Amazon.com, www.amazon.com

ⓘ Barnes & Noble, 800-843-2665, www.bn.com

ⓘ Your local bookstore may carry the book or can order it for you

Price: $10–$25

Easy if your loved one is
♥ *long distance*
♥ *local*

Delivered by retailer

Pack it yourself

Holidays

Here are some days you can celebrate with your loved ones. If the day always falls on a certain date, it's indicated.

New Year's Day—January 1
Happy Mew Years for Cats Day—January 2
Fruitcake Toss Day—January 7
Penguin Awareness Day—January 14
Martin Luther King's Birthday
National Hugging Day—January 21
National Compliment Day—January 25
Groundhog Day—February 2
Wear Red Day—February 3
White Shirt Day—February 11
Mardi Gras
Ash Wednesday
Chinese New Year
Lincoln's Birthday—February 12
Valentine's Day—February 14
Washington's Birthday—February 22
Beer Day—March 1
National Be Heard Day—March 7
St Patrick's Day—March 17
First Day of Spring—March 20
As Young as You Feel Day—March 22
April Fool's Day—April 1
Palm Sunday
Good Friday
Easter

Passover
Walk On Your Wild Side Day—April 12
Administrative Professionals' Day
     (Formerly Secretaries' Day)—April 21
Earth Day—April 22
May Day—May 1
Cinco De Mayo—May 5
V E Day—May 8
Mother's Day
International Day of Families—May 15
Armed Forces Day—May 20
National Maritime Day—May 22
Memorial Day
Donut Day—June 3
D Day—June 6
Flag Day—June 14
Father's Day
Summer Solstice/Howl at the Moon Day
First Day of Summer— June 21
Independence Day—July 4
National Ice Cream Day—July 16
National Parents' Day—July 23
Take Your Houseplant for a Walk Day—July 27
Girlfriends' Day—August 1
Happiness Happens Day—August 8
National Underwear Day—August 9
Best Friends' Day—August 15
V J Day—September 2
Labor Day—September 4
Fortune Cookie Day—September 13
Respect for the Aged Day (Japan)

National POW/MIA Recognition Day—September 15
Talk Like a Pirate Day—September 19
Harvest Moon
First Day of Autumn—September 22
Ramadan
Rosh Hashanah
VFW Day—September 29
International Eat an Apple Day
International Day of Older Persons—October 1
Yom Kippur
Mad Hatter Day—October 6
Columbus Day
National Bosses' Day—November 16
Mother-In-Law Day—October 22
Halloween—Oct. 31
All Souls Day/All Saints Day—November 1
Sadie Hawkins Day—November 4
Veterans Day—November 11
World Kindness Day—November 13
Mickey Mouse Day—November 18
Have a Bad Day Day—November 19
Thanksgiving Day—fourth Thursday of November
Saint Nicholas Day—December 6
Pearl Harbor Day—December 7
Day of the Horse—December 9
Hanukkah
Humbug Day / First Day of Winter—December 21
Christmas Eve—December 24
Christmas Day—December 25
Boxing Day—December 26
New Year's Eve—December 31

If you enjoy the fun holidays (Talk Like a Pirate Day, Fortune Cookie Day, etc.) go to brownielocks.com/month2.html for a monthly listing of all the goofy days for high jinks with your loved one. Also enjoy the book Celebrate Today *by John Kremer, which has 3,200 holidays in it.*

Bibliography

Abramson, Alexis. *The Caregiver's Survival Handbook: How to Care for Your Aging Parent Without Losing Yourself.* New York: The Berkley Publishing Group. 2004.

Barg, Gary. *The Fearless Caregiver: How to Get the Best Care for Your Loved One and Still Have a Life of Your Own.* First edition. Herndon, VA: Capital Books, Inc. 2003.

Beresford, Larry. *The Hospice Handbook.* First edition. Boston: Little, Brown & Company. 1993.

Berman, Claire. *Caring for Yourself While Caring for Your Aging Parents: How to Help, How to Survive.* New York: Henry Holt and Company. 1997.

Brandt, Avrene L., Ph.D. *Caregiver's Reprieve.* San Luis Obispo, CA: Impact Publishers, Inc. 1997.

Callanan, Maggie and Patricia Kelley. *Final Gifts: Understanding the Special Awareness, Needs and Communications of the Dying.* New York: Bantam Books. 1993.

Cilley, Marla. *Sink Reflections.* New York: Bantam Publishing. 2002.

Delehanty, Hugh and Elinor Ginzler. *Caring for Your Aging Parents.* New York: Sterling Publishing Co., Inc. 2005.

Feil, Naomi. *The Validation Breakthrough.* Fifth edition. Baltimore: Health Professions Press, Inc. 1997.

Focus on the Family Physicians Resource Council. *Caring for Aging Loved Ones.* Edited by Linda Piepenbrink. Wheaton, IL: Tyndale House Publishers, Inc. 2002.

Fourteen Friends' Guide to Elder-Caring. New York: Broadway Books. 1999.

Gould, Jean. *Dutiful Daughters: Caring for Our Parents as They Grow Old.* First edition. Edited by Jean Gould. Seattle: Seal Press. 1999.

Greenberg, Vivian E. *Respecting Your Limits When Caring For Aging Parents.* San Francisco: Jossey-Bass, Publishers, Inc. 1998.

Heath, Angela. *Long Distance Caregiving: A Survival Guide for Far Away Caregivers.* Fourth edition. San Luis Obispo, CA: Impact Publishers, Inc. 1996.

Lebow, Grace and Barbara Kane with Irwin Lebow. *Coping with Your Difficult Older Parent: A Guide for Stressed-Out Children* . New York: Avon Books. 1999.

Mace, Nancy L., M.A. and Peter V. Rabins, M.D., MPH. *The 36-Hour Day.* New York: Warner Books, Inc. 1981.

Markin, R.E., Ph.D. *The Alzheimer's Cope Book.* New York: Carol Publishing Group. 1992.

Medved, Denise Sullivan. *The Tiny Kitchen.* First Edition. Annandale, Virginia: Tiny Kitchen Publishing. 2001.

Morse, Sarah and Donna Quinn Robbins. *Moving Mom and Dad!* Second edition. Petaluma, CA: Lanier Publishing International, Ltd.. Center City, MI: 1991.

Samples, Pat and Diane Larsen and Marvin Larsen. *Self-Care for Caregivers: A Twelve Step Approach.* Center City, MI: Hazeldon. 1991.

Susik, D. Helen, M.A. *Hiring Home Caregivers.* Second edition. San Luis Obispo, CA: Impact Publishing Co., Inc. 1995.

The Hartford. *At the Crossroads: A Guide to Alzheimer's Disease, Dementia & Driving.* Southington, CT. 2005.

Williams, Gene B. and Patie Kay. *The Caregiver's Manual.* New York: Carol Publishing Group. 1995.

Zeiger, Genie. *How I Find Her: A Mother's Dying and a Daughter's Life.* Santa Fe, NM: Sherman Asher Publishing. 2001.

About the Author

Jane Monachelli is an Arizona Licensed Professional Counselor who specializes in grief counseling and relationship and couples therapy. She has had a private practice in the Phoenix area for 25 years.

A member of the American Counseling Association, the American Mental Health Association, the Arizona Mental Health Counselors Association and the Arizona Counselors Association, Jane also provides consulting services for Intergroup of Arizona, Patients Choice, Syntex, and project Headstart. Jane has provided services for the John C. Casey Foundation and is involved with the Wellness Foundation, a charitable organization that offers free services to single mothers. She is a trained member of the mental health disaster team for the American Red Cross and was involved in work with the Katrina survivors.

Jane is a popular speaker and has appeared on radio and TV, covering subjects such as "Women and Depression," "Codependency and Recovery," "Samaritan Presents: Women in Mid-life" and "Holidays and Rituals—Self Esteem."

She lives in Phoenix, Arizona, with her husband, Ron, where she delights in her role as grandmother.

Now It's Your Turn

If you didn't see your favorite ideas in the book, please share them with us, and we'll share them with others! Just give us as much information as you can below. If we use your tip in a future book, on our Web site or anywhere else, we'll acknowledge you and send you a free copy of any book in which it's included.

Just photocopy this page and mail it to:

Jane Monachelli

c/o Helping House

17 E. Orange Dr.

Phoenix AZ 85012-1427

My idea _____

_____

_____

_____

It can be purchased at

Store name: _____

Store phone number: _____

Store Web site: _____

My name _____

Address _____

City_____ State____ Zip _____

Phone number _____

Email _____

Thank you.